ABOUT

In 2017, corporationpop emerged as a result of Northern beat poet Elise Hadgraft's late night drinking sessions in a suburban kitchen. Although she no longer drinks, she continues to produce and release music under the moniker of corporationpop.

A look back at ten years of procrastination, 'Now There Are No More Love Songs' is the closest Elise Hadgraft ever wants to get to a best of. It includes some notable performance pieces from an often volatile and divisive career, as well as a hodgepodge of corporationpop lyrics and a few long forgotten relics.

#HYSTPoet

Special thanks to godisanewt for the original fanzine featured in this collection.

Should it be of interest, the entire corporationpop back catalogue can be downloaded for free from: **https://corporationpopband.bandcamp.com/**

corporationpop
Now There Are No More Love Songs

VERVE
POETRY PRESS
BIRMINGHAM

PUBLISHED BY VERVE POETRY PRESS
https://vervepoetrypress.com
mail@vervepoetrypress.com

All rights reserved
© 2020 /Elise Hadgraft/corporationpop

The right of Elise Hadgraft to be identified as author of this work has been asserted in accordance with section 77 of the Copyright, Designs and Patents Act 1988.

No part of this work may be reproduced, stored or transmitted in any form or by any means, graphic, electronic, recorded or mechanical, without the prior written permission of the publisher.

FIRST PUBLISHED OCT 2020

Printed and bound in the UK
by ImprintDigital, Exeter

ISBN: 978-1-912565-43-6

Cover Design: Elise Hadgraft

CONTENTS

Introduction

Seven Miles South	11
Sweets	13
You Write Songs	15
I Wanna Wear Your Clothes	17
Salamander Street	19
Sylvia Suspects	21
The Poem Which Came To Be Known As 'Affirmations'	23
Lucille	24
Frownies™	27
You Promised If I Put This In, You'd Buy My Book	29
Megan	31
Trying 2 Make It Work	33
The First Poem I Wrote On My Return To Manchester	36
Scraps	39
Doctor, Doctor	40
If I Should Die This Winter	42

Fanzine

INTRODUCTION

Dear Reader,

This is not a poem. No, really, it's not. I know it's not a poem because I wrote it (quite specifically) to be 'not a poem'. You're still reading it in the poetry voice, aren't you? You fucking maverick. That doesn't make it a poem though. You can put a wobble in your voice and a catch in your throat and gesticulate and gaze and slam cadence the living shit out of this and it will remain as obstinately un-poem as it was at the very beginning of its not being a poem.

For an awfully long time, I was not a poet.

I desperately wanted to be. I've always loved poetry and during my first week of university (all the way back in 2008) I finally had courage enough to take myself to a poetry night. If I had known then what I know now, I'd have told a significantly larger amount of people in that room to shove their opinions firmly up their arse. If you've heard the stories, then you know that I would go on to do exactly this, not too long afterwards, but I'd be playing it for laughs by then.

See, my early poetry was not good. My early poetry, like a potter's first go at the wheel, was about as artistically pleasing as it was useful...but the mess it made was fun to watch.

In the years that followed, I learned to rely on that mess. I revelled in it. Nobody's laundry was dirtier than mine and each night I'd peg it up proudly across the stage and loudly proclaim the origin of each and every stain. The laughs rolled in. Deservedly so, a sad clown is still a clown and a sad clown who produces her own theme music and regularly takes her kit off is a hot commodity. I got a little better at writing, as you do with repetition, but without ever quite realising how, I lost myself into a caricature.

I have been asked since if I regret the first decade of my career, and for a little while I probably did. As such, compiling the pieces for 'Now There Are No More Love Songs' has been a strange process, but ultimately a cathartic one.

These are the poems which taught me I could make a room full of drunk people shut up and listen. The poems which opened doors and sometimes closed them again. The poems which fostered friendships and rivalries and all the best bits of being a live artist. These poems have made people cry or laugh or leave or never turn up in the first place. They've been recorded, ripped off, badly transcribed and circulated at dinner parties I wasn't invited to. These poems are as much yours as they are mine.

This is not a poem

And I am still not much of a poet

But one day I hope that I might be.

Now There Are No More Love Songs

Seven Miles South
from the EP 'Meet Me By The Viaduct'

Welcome to Stockport,
Pull up a piece of re-refurbished precinct,
We've been wasting council money
Since nineteen sixty-three.
This is Stockport
'Hub of industry'
Where pubs become nurseries
And the streets are paved with puns
From Robinson's Brewery,
We're the wrong side of the Pennines
But the right side of the Mersey.

Suburbia is calling
To those who want to listen,
Where drinking starts at four
In your mother's prefab kitchen.
So, meet me by the viaduct
And I'll let you take my picture,
With the camera that you stole
From your old sixth form teacher.

Welcome to Stockport,
Spiritual home of universally low self-esteem,
Twee industrial history
And poverty safaris.
Although we're quietly optimistic
Raised these kids on McVitie's biscuits,
Frustrated ambition and
Resistance to cold –

I can't come out Friday night
'Cause my brother's got my coat

And suburbia is calling
To those who want to listen,
Where drinking starts at four
In your mother's prefab kitchen.
So, meet me by the viaduct
And I'll let you take my picture,
With the camera that you stole
From your old sixth form teacher.

Seven miles south of town
Run down
Red brick
Kick the shit out of strangers
Though strangeness sustains us
This is
This is
This is Stockport
And it's calling
To those who want to listen,
Where drinking starts at four
In your mother's prefab kitchen.
So, meet me by the viaduct
And I'll let you take my picture,
With the camera that you stole
From your old sixth form teacher.

Sweets

It begins with sweets.

Woolworths in the 90's.
A training facility for
Small time thieves
Chancers
Future local characters
Like me.
Those of us who see
An opportunity, seized
Between the foam shrimp
And the jelly beans.
There's no technique.
It's not about skill
Or the thrill of
Self-fulfilling prophecy.
Stealing sweets comes as
Easily, as logically
As breathing. And
My feelings for you are
Handfuls of Black Jacks,
Palms sticky from taking
Things I shouldn't have.
White chocolate mice,
Hearing you recite poetry
Gets me going
Like Dolly Mixtures
Before they got rid of
The artificial colourings.

You are jelly rings
Red lips
Pixy Stix
Pocketed to a soundtrack of 'Razzmatazz' –
Jazzles!
As bad for my teeth as
My self-esteem, because
I don't actually need you and
You don't notice me.
Oblivious
As the neatly pressed
Polyester dressed
Shop front security.
I'd wager I could run naked
Between the fried eggs
And the bonbons
Before you cottoned on
To my existence.
Though I'll still listen.
Still look adoringly
From a distance.
Still consider the viability
Of stealing.

But emotions aren't easy,
Not like sweets.

You Write Songs
from the EP 'The Chester Road Demos'

You write songs like I recite shopping lists
Staving off forgetfulness
With bread
And milk
And washing-up liquid
It's your turn to do the dishes
Stretched as we are between
Sex, asthma and domesticity
Sex City citizens
So far from sexy
We're constantly walking
Since public transport is a luxury we can't afford this week
And wine
And cheese
Four pounds seventy on the meter to see me through until
Tuesday
Even heat
Even heat's a pipe dream.

You write songs like I boil kettles
Fill baths by the pint and buy
Only the essentials
And apples
And toilet roll
And soapbox Britpop singles
You write songs like I put clingfilm on windows
Well-honed dexterity
Three degrees above freezing
You write songs like sweets.

You write songs like sweets old ladies fed me
On suburban streets
In nineteen ninety-five.
You write songs like songwriters lie
You write songs like songwriters lie
You write songs like songwriters lie.

I Wanna Wear Your Clothes
(He did not deserve this poem)

I wanna wear your clothes.
I wanna wear your clothes and compose an album
Pose in each, individual item
Babydoll let's leave the lights on
'Cause since we met
I can't seem to get dressed alone,
I just wanna wear your clothes

And I'll start with your shirts.
So that every day at work
You'll know that I was in them first,
The curve of my breasts pressed
Where your chest rests now,
They fit you better anyhow
But I still wanna wear your clothes.

You own more coats than
Any man I've ever known,
Each doorframe overflows and
I've not slept in my own bed yet this weekend
'Cause I've been skipping nights at home
In my pursuit to wear your clothes –
I'd walk a mile in your shoes and there's
A few pairs to get through –
Wear new grooves in the leather
Where we don't quite fit together
'Til we do.
And I do wanna wear your clothes

Raid your wardrobes
Beg and borrow
Steal if I've got to, 'til the photos don't matter.
'Cause there's not a jumper or a jacket you can look at
Without seeing me
Superimposed.

I've given you my heart,
But I just wanna wear your clothes.

Salamander Street

The first time I saw you
(In person, not photos)
You were walking towards me
Down Salamander Street
In the heat of Edinburgh's
Steady ascent into summer.
Sun at your back, and a 1970's
Sheepskin jacket slung casually
Over one shoulder.

You must have been chuffing roasting.

From that moment
I was hopelessly yours.
It took FOUR WEEKS to
Convince you to sleep with me.
But, touching the
Impeccably formed contours
Of your body, spread
Across a single bed in Marchmont,
As 5am light filtered in
Through too-thin parchment blinds, was
Without question
Worth the indignity of pleading.

You are still the most beautiful man
I've ever seen and I told you ceaselessly.
A steady stream of
Heavy-handed compliments,

I've not always been as good at this.
Called you my 'Adonis in loungewear'.
Just felt lucky to be there, really
Couldn't quite believe
You'd so much as given me
The time of day.
A man straight out of teenage me's
Formative sex dreams:
Who cooked
Who read *real* books
Who regularly paused when we fucked
To quote inappropriate Pulp lyrics.
Mother, I can never come home again.
You were perfect
And I was, well,
Me.

We parted ways in January,
Five days after New Year,
And though I'm several bodies clear
Of your memory
I still routinely see you naked
Behind my eyelids –
Around 5am – when
Our mutual aversion
To functional curtains
Silently lets the light get in.

Sylvia Suspects
(The rarely seen companion piece to 'Sylvia Suburban')

Sylvia suspects it's time to shake things up a bit.
Gets dressed,
Does her makeup every morning
To the playlist she's had on since 2006
With limited additions.
Makes room for new albums by Jarvis
But that's about it.
Still wouldn't kick him out of bed.
Is becoming quite accomplished
At impressions,
Might just pass for human,
Does an excellent rendition of 'Lipgloss'
When she's drunk enough.
Doesn't get out the house much,
Much prefers her bathroom and
An audience of one.

Sylvia suspects they've got her sussed.
Couldn't tell you quite who 'they' was –
But knows enough to know,
You know?
Sleeps with her phone under her pillow,
Just in case.
Checks applications on rotation.
Places her faith
In validation from strangers.

Sylvia suspects the lies she tells herself are
Gaining on her.
Only so far Valencia filter can take her,
Only so much habitual behaviour,
Before she concedes
To a caricature
Of a character
From books that she no longer reads.

Sylvia suspects she'll always be a shop girl.
Never fuck Jarvis Cocker.
Never amount to much, really.
Still reads Rush-Hour Crush
On the bus to work weekly,
Plays the National Lottery,
Regularly lets horoscopes ruin her day.
Sylvia is susceptible that way,
A superstitious Millennial that way.

Sylvia suspects no one's really listening.
Blames her failings on:
Private education
The television that raised her
And tits, nature never thought fit to bring.

Would have been a singer,
If only she could sing.

The Poem Which Came To Be Known As 'Affirmations'

I am no man's Yoko Ono!
Birkin, Sedgwick or Brigitte Bardot.
Liza Doolittle?
Too little too late.
I were born an artist
Not Factory made, or
Test tube babe of some Svengali:
"I'll make you a star, love
Just hold this for me."

A little old for an ingénue
Mouth like a sailor
Long in't tooth, but
I wouldn't do my yoof again
Take 'measures' to preserve what's left
Or set my face at twenty-eight
Blow this joint, and
In my place
Leave nostalgic snapshots
(Forever young)
The 'just over twenty-seven' club.

I am no man's bit of fluff
I have my universal truth...
Life's wasted on the fucking stupid,
And those who try to bottle youth.

Lucille

Lucille,
I know you feel
Inadequate.
These dancefloor anorexics
Are packed in like matchsticks
Digging your soft edges
In this inner-city bedsit
Listening to the best of 'The Smiths'.

Some girls are bigger and
Better than this,
But not us.

We missed the last bus back to the suburbs,
Though I heard
Pretty girls drink free
At nostalgic, indie parties –
And you were so arty
So painfully indie
Back in Salford '03.

Little Lucie,
Skipping breakfast
Skipping lessons
Still dating that musician who denied your existence
To his mates
Girl afraid
You're better off rid
His band were shit, anyway.

Who knew you'd make it to twenty-eight?
Or thirty?
Or thirty-three?
And still be part of the same old scene
Where stories of our glory days
Feed our insecurities about ageing
Singing
Hang the DJ
Hang the DJ
Hang the DJ
Hang the DJ...

Lucille,
I know you feel
Nervous.
Now the kids all dress
Like they bought their threads
At charity shops
On purpose.
You've actually had this skirt since 1996
It's not vintage
It's just used
Like you,
Which might sound harsh
But Golden Age thinking is fucking farcical.

To the girl in the 1970's shirt,
Why wait around for the reunion tour
When there are bad cover versions
Here
Now
Tunelessly shouted in inner-city bedsits

Where the dancefloor anorexics
Are packed in like matchsticks
And you don't give a shit
If you haven't got a stitch to wear tonight,
'Cause you're going out
Regardless.

Frownies™

You may be surprised to hear
I don't get told I should smile more,
What I do get told is:

"You should frown less,"
He said.
"You should
Frown
Less.
This moody disposition upsets me,
Less sexy than resting bitch face,
It betrays your age.
How can you expect me to stay
Faithful
When the windows to your soul
Are so unwholesome in frame?
Babe,
Your body is a playground
But there's just no getting round
That ploughed furrow
Sea wall shallow's sheer drop
Craggy rock on your cliff face.
It's a shame –
Pretty girl like you,
Unduly ravaged
By the grasping hands of time,
I'd suggest a quick fix
But you know how it is
Bitches just can't take a compliment."

You might imagine this
Is the bit in the narrative
Where I kick to the pavement
My misogynist, wank-stain bae.
Tell him to away
To his mum's spare room,
PornHub or Xtube or
Whatever the fuck it is you do
When you're clearly not nearly
Mature enough to touch
A real woman,
Wouldn't you?

If only that were true.

Instead each night I go to bed
With paper on my forehead.
Paper on my forehead
That sets solid
To prevent frowning.
To tone down,
Smooth out,
Make the middle of my brows
As crease free
As my dignity
Before he ever fucking told me
"You should frown less."

You Promised If I Put This In, You'd Buy My Book

We say it's like Romeo and Juliet.
Except, instead of Montagues and Capulets,
We get comedians and poets.
And I know it's not unusual
For artists
Whose partners grow sick of
The late-night gig circuit, its
Concentric social circles, to go
"Fuck this for a game of soldiers
I'm dating solely other artists!"
But, I'm your first.
Artist, not partner, Jesus.
Is this as weird for you
As it is for me?
This.
This bit.
Where we ardently avoid going to each other's gigs
As if being shit (and we're all a bit shit sometimes)
Would somehow dull the shine.

A mutual acquaintance
Shamelessly told you I was funny.
I'm not funny.
Not professionally,
Not in the new-wrinkle-inducing way

You're funny.
I'm 'comedy is tragedy plus time'
Occasionally rhyming
With emphasis on the tragedy.
You catch your flies with honey,
I mostly succeed in not crying audibly on stage.

It's strange,
You call me by my last name
And I don't hate it.

Maybe next week
You'll come and see this.

Megan
(Performed only once, to a half-filled room, with a fever of 104°)

Megan is no spring chicken
So, she knows some things like:
Letting go is sometimes the only way of moving on –
She isn't wrong.
Navigating ex-girlfriends
Is like misreading chest pains,
They suggest you might be dying
Whilst you see only concrete confirmation
You're alive.
Denial of mortality
Is simply *denial*
And she can see you're in deep,
Are a weak swimmer,
Contemplates tossing a life saver
But you're too much of a tosser and suffering
Is its own reward
Or something.
To her this is a 'teachable moment'.
I might have mentioned, Megan
Knows her shit
Knows the difference
Knows that if it
Looks like a cunt and
Quacks like a cunt
It probably is one.

Megan does not accept the term 'friends'
In reference to women you've had your penis in,

Based on empirical evidence.
Megan is not convinced
You're a 'big fish in a small pond'
And not just pond scum
She happened to have stepped on.
Megan is not nearly so green.
Is fluent in deceit,
The way it blooms across your body
Like braille.
Will not be reduced to
Single White Female-ing
Jane fucking Birkin
Again.
Megan is just Megan,
And Megan
Is getting out.
Will be waving as you're drowning,
Shouting
"Who's the failure now?
Yeah.
Who's the fucking failure now?"

Trying 2 Make It Work
(Written for, and originally featuring the musical stylings of, Clingfilm)

Most nights
She watches herself cry
In his bureau mirror.
It's never 'pretty' per se
But symmetrically framed
The contours of her face are
French New Wave grace
On a council estate budget.
She scrunches her eyes
Wrings them dry and
Calls her mother.

God loves a trier,
And it's trying her patience
Trying to make this
Second rate sex
A relationship.
She's yet to get to Paris
On his Butlins budget
But is trying
To make it
Work.

More fool her.
Innit.

In the cinematic adaptation
Of her bullshit existence

Night-time, red eyed reflections
Will be realised by indie directors and
Uplit with the neon glow of a mobile phone
It'll be
So
Fucking
Art.

Though she knows
She tries too hard.

In years to come,
She imagines some young aficionados
Will compose love letters
To her flat chest against
Own brand bedding and attest
Her performance was
Wasted on him.

She is Godard's complex feminine,
A Northern bedsit heroine, like
Wes Anderson did the narrative
But Shane Meadows picked the setting.

Hitchcock blonde
To a half-cocked lover
Wake up
Wake up
Wake up you boring...

Cut to morning

As it dawns on her
That sunlight looks better
With the curtains closed, and
This bed would feel less empty
If she were laid in it
Alone.

She goes home.

The First Poem I Wrote On My Return To Manchester
(...and now refuse to perform)

As I pass, you'll ask me
"Spare some change, duck?"
And I will look you straight in the eye,
Without even tasting the lie, reply
"Sorry love, just enough for my bus."
Make to walk away
Patting my back pocket
When you'll say,
"No worries. Have a great night."
That.
That is when the affliction hits
My chest constricts and
I am gripped with the knowledge that
You know.
You know.
I've got a fair few quid surplus to my requirements
It is not much
I am by no means flush, but
Mainstream media has bred in me
Such mistrust
That I would begrudge you
The price of a cup of tea
In bloody Starbucks.

This could be any city.
You
Any ethnicity, gender or age

Because poverty
Unlike me
Doesn't discriminate.
But this is the place of my birth,
And now I am angry.
Angry,
That despite my leftist doctrine of beliefs
I still have a subconscious need for proof.
Angry,
That I will weigh you
Against your 24,999 (and rising) counterparts
Just to justify holding on to my change tonight.

Though I know I could assuage my conscience,
Leave my offering by the Palace
Of coffee and a sandwich,
Because I have seen you –
With those Styrofoam cups
Of people's guilt
Lined up
Six-deep
Between you.

It is not enough.

Maybe I should say, "Fuck the bus!"
Sit down and discuss this
Or better yet,
Regress to the moment that it happened,
Be there to greet you on the doorstep with a blanket
Tell you, "I know you can't go back, but please..."

Though the governmental assistance you need
No longer exists, so
Regardless of time-travelling altruists
You will still sleep rough tonight
And every night after this.

I am powerless.

I turn back,
Place two quid into the hat at your feet
And then flee
Catching my bus with ease, but
Travelling home feeling
Hollow
Knowing that tomorrow
As I pass, you'll ask me
"Spare some change, duck?"

Scraps

There are no more love songs.
But you left me poems in pockets
of coats I don't wear often, so
three months post-breakup
I could mistake carefully creased
poetry for money and feel
both skint and lonely – now
There are no more love songs.

Doctor, Doctor

I may have got the talent
But I never got the tits
They say 'dance like no one's watching'
And that's 'cause no one is
With a gift for words like this
You need a face to match
Except when I fell out the ugly tree
I got caught on that branch
And I've been hanging somewhere in between
Since nineteen ninety-eight
For my face to grow into my nose
Or nose into my face
Let's say the problem's not all that
It's stature or my voice
A tone-deaf tosspot toddler
Who will not share her toys!
Aren't I such a sport?
Of course, I'm just one of the blokes
If you don't wait for the punchline
You'll never get the joke
We misplaced just one chromosome
Your girl can't get the parts
To make a living just like you
A poor man's Cooper Clarke.

A poor man's Cooper Clarke
She said
A poor man's Cooper Clarke

Doctor, doctor
I'd rather be dead
Than a poor man's Cooper Clarke.

If I Should Die This Winter
(A hastily made addition)

In six months,
When the numbers get crunched,
Over brunch with a friend
(A friend you made because you underestimated
How isolating isolation could be)
You will see
In that stream of data
The indeterminable nature of luck.

You are lucky.

One of many.

Joint winners in the randomly selected
'Genetic, locational, health care specifications' lottery.
Do not for one second believe the fusilli
You elbow barged an old lady to retrieve
Saved you.
It is statistically more likely to have been
An angel
A lack of petrol
An instinctual decision to not brave Tesco
An untaken left
Or right
Being tired but not rubbing your eyes
Antibacterial wipes
(The three times you ever remembered to use them)
Losing Monopoly...
Leading to your not speaking to your family for two weeks

A narrowly avoided sneeze
'Getting healthy', whatever that means
Making 2020 the year you stuck to an exercise regime
The bravery of other people.

People who may not have been so lucky.

In six months,
When the numbers get crunched,
Over brunch with a friend
(A friend you made because you underestimated
How isolating isolation could be)
You will see
In that stream of data
The indeterminable nature of luck
And you will weep for the unlucky.

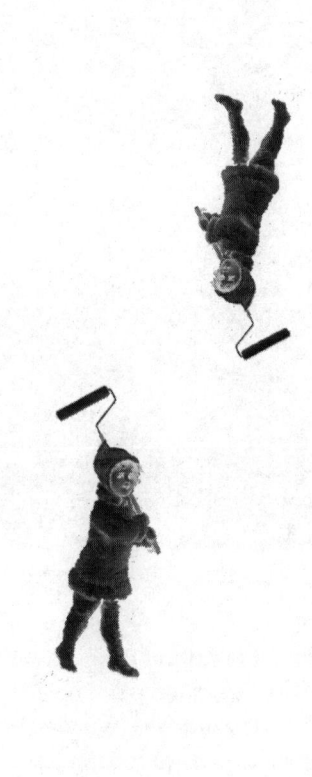

My Papa bloomed brightest in his
English country rose garden,
But when winter alighted
On the edges of his petals
He did not fight it.

And in each piece of bindweed
I am too cold or tired or busy
To remove
I fail you.

This book is dedicated to my Papa. Your repertoire was limited, but your voice was always the loudest in the room.

His rose garden is
A fragrant display of vandalism:
Each plant the ill-gotten gains
Of days spent in stately homes.
He knows the secret names,
Translates them for me,
Heritage breeds and
Specialist species - curated
For this single space.
He tells me it's a waste.
That we must liberate them.
I am his accomplice
(Trusted with freshly sharpened snips)
Though little bigger
Than the more established bushes.
We take a dozen cuttings.
Enough to fill the pockets
Of a pink cotton coat
I've long since outgrown.

Back home he teaches me of loss,
How not every stem can root
But those that do...
Those that do will thrive.
A fight to survive can make us.

You are possessed of an
Unexpected clumsiness,
As though your legs –
Having perfected dancing –
Found themselves affronted
By other forms of movement.

I will shroud you in music.
So, when you sing
(And you do)
It will shake the very foundations
Of the places
I am yet to take you.

You are amazing.

Complex,
Conch shell strength
Enveloped by softness.
There is no bit of skin, stretched
Porcelain pale,
Over this warrior princess
I would not kiss. Yet
You can list your imperfections
By heart and (armed
With well-practiced rhetoric)
I have seen you demolish the
Numerous cities of yourself.

You do not need my help.

A pretty face may
Launch a thousand ships,
But empires have folded with
A single sentence uttered
From your Cupid's bow lips.
Lips I have bitten,
Rendered in crimson,
Tasted the iron of
Ancient civilisations and
Whispered my devotion in
Languages long dead.

Little goddess.

The Very Last Love Song

You waited twenty-eight years
To receive a love song.

You've written dozens.
Watched sparks erupt
Behind lovers' eyes,
Made grown men cry,
Manipulated time,
Stolen moments
In ways a photo never could.

You are good.

You are good at poetry,
And love, because
You have studied
Extensively.

Books have always been
Your best friends.
This does not make you 'quirky',
It makes you:
Well read
Intelligent
Engaging
Leaves me wishing
I could dress as pages from your favourites
That maybe you would bless me
With the graces you do paper.

Mount Olympus is Empty

Love of my old lover,

I know you see these. Poetry, steeped like weak tea in lazy metaphor, let me pour you a cup. We can speak candidly. Mount Olympus is empty. I do not hate you as you must hate me, do not feel guilty.

We both knelt freely, loved him honestly, if differently.

But these knees were not made to crawl, to sit patiently or passively.

Unlike yours – my body does not lie so easy underneath.

Do not feel guilty. Keep him, please. Tread lightly and sleep easy. Scan the skies until you're blind. Read widely.

Your intuition is a gift, and it was right.

Believe me.

It is said that names hold power:
So, cower now
Round your apple trees and golden fleeces,
In deepest seas and secret places,
For I have seen your faces.
I know your names.
You will not escape this fate.

A History of Dragons

Dearest one,
It pains me that you must slay these dragons,
Their weathered wingspan has too long arced
Across the skies of your childhood.

No good has ever come of magic.

Be done with it quickly.
Cleanly.
Resign these beasts to the sediment of memory,
To the dinosaurs and deities,

We'll pack the bodies tightly.
Summer holiday suitcase full
I'll pull the zip
If you weigh it down

Down

We'll drown ourselves in unmapped depths.
The Hydra has many heads
And each will resemble the face of some
Faceless shade.

The names remain stuck,
Unuttered by a mother's tongue,
But there are teeth and talons enough
To pry them from your childish lungs
In an exultant rush of breath.

The Pygmalion's Girl

"She was made to be looked at..."

You said 'she was made'
As if your gifted hands
Had worked the clay
Like a labour of love:
Roughed her surface,
Shaped each facet,
Added curves
To reflect your image,
Then polished her difference
Smooth.

See, she is a vision of Eden.

You but not you,
Not equal,
Engrave your initials on the base of her heel.

Same, but not *the same*.

She may have been made to be looked at
But it was you who rendered her lame.

Minotaurticulturist

My mother solves problems.

Her green thumbs did not come
Naturally, like me.
She steadfastly curated them,
Planted late, awaited them
With grim determination,
I have seen her raise the dead.

She ties her thread to no labyrinth.

Instead, 'the cactus resurrected'
In a two-bedroom terraced
You could never get lost in.
Each window ledge is a garden
Of unkillable resilience,
She favours the succulents.

No nonsense. High maintenance.

Traitorous babes to raise
And named so strangely,
As though the gods gazed
Only briefly but grew weary,
In Crete they call me Asterion.

My mother solves problems.
I am my mother's son.

Mistress Midas

Perhaps to you
I am a vein of gold
In some cold and desolate cave?

Though you crave what I provide
You will not abide
To stay.

You visit daily
Admire my 'mining capabilities'
Lay wooden beams to hold me
(Fixed screaming)
And send the team in to chip my teeth.

                        We make rings
                For the women
        Who are not
Me.

Brother of Monsters

I cannot fault your optimism:
That in,
One by one,
Dragging up my demons
And drowning them...

(As though furtive burdens
Might pass easily as kittens,
Bagged and buried on a Greek beach)

That in,
One by one,
Dragging up my demons
And drowning them...
You can save me.

Brother, please.
These secrets are no meek and mewling house pets.
Your shores?
No threat.
Open waters?
Potential.

Your little sister is filled to the brim
With *Anguilla rostrata*,
Black eels,
And she will swim.

Demophon's Burden

I have lived between breaths
Cheeks puffed in petulance
I gulped down love and held it in
I am selfish
Aether driven, yet
You could be forgiven
For reading me innocent
A red-faced infant
Engaged in a painless game
Of temperament.

I have lived.

But there are burning silences
Between
Breaths
That ever see me bested.

Poem to Hylas

In some
Far flung
Alternate history
We are sixteen:
It is summer and
You are walking me
To my mother's
Down streets that,
In reality,
You will not see
For nearly twenty years.

Wishing you were here.

Evening heat creeps
From freckled cheeks
To freshly pierced ears
And your hand,
Strange weathered by lands
It is yet to travel,
Unravels the mystery of mine.

Time
It has been said
Is of no consequence to projections
So, we occupy my childhood bedroom
Like smoke

When it is over you open the window.

Pyromania

DO NOT TRUST ME WITH MATCHES.

Look at these hands!
I am a patchwork
Of brandings,
Self-inflicted.

I take needles to my blisters
Drink accelerant for breakfast
Possess a tinderbox heart.

You are domestic,
Hestia tended,
A home hearth.

DO NOT TRUST ME.

I will empty your embers on the bedsheets,
Blow sweetly
And let this fire start.

Hero Gets a Regrettable Tattoo

They say I have
'One of those faces' –
The kind that betrays
My every emotion.

Our hearts seem as if an ocean
And unbeknownst to them
Shame rages below,
Tempest blown,
On slowly shrinking shoulders.

Lifeboats
Gain holes
With each passing moment.

Ink on skin.

Lover, I am drowning.

Arachne

You are a prisoner.

And you'd do well to remember
That gilded cages are
Betrayed by iron hearts and
Sweetly smiling guards
Who bind your arms
With the finest woven lies
They tie you gently
Let you see how each knot
(One under, one over, one-upped)
Increases the intricacy.

Your body is a bridal lace
You have married this deceit.

The Mother and the Mystic

"Contrary,"
He said,
"A three headed
She-devil,
I never know
Which witch
I'm going to get!"

Tender-hearted.
Two torches
Are excessive
For this short wick
Candle,
Though I handle
My spirits
Well.

Ring the bell.
I'll read your cards,
Spin you a yarn,
To hell in a
Handknit cardigan.

You say Heck'-ate
I say Heh-cah'-tay

Let's call the whole thing done.

Lunesta

Hypnos brings me
Bad dreams,
A sleepless symphony
Of discomforts, he
Rolls us over in
Sweat-drenched sheets.
Our borrowed bed
Creaks.
With each movement,
I will you would
Stay still...
But we, a dishabille of
Ill-fitting limbs,
Lie restless.

Come morning,
I will forget this.

Digital Aphrodite

Call me 'goddess'.
Validate my vanity.
Send me pictures,
Missives signed with
Three kisses –
Type them one handed,
Sweaty palmed,
Is it the distance
That makes it hard?

Are you devoted?

Will you worship only
At the apex of my filtered thighs?

When you dream of me naked
Am I black and white?

A Hollywood siren
With little girl's eyes.

Lament for a Fallen God

Dionysus
Drinks himself warm
On the corner
Of Oxford Street.
His blanket green,
Like vine leaves,
From the recent
Rain.
It's been six days and
Hunger
Paves the way
To delirium.
He speaks in tongues,
Mumbles songs of
Old gods.
His old dog,
Lost to madness,
Shivers.
Secrets drip from
Cracked lips and
City commuters
Trip from transport
To computer
Deaf
Mute pressed
They do not listen.

Dionysus drinks himself
To winter.

Cassandra

They do not tell you
In fairy tales
That heartbreak has a taste:

It is
Gin, slims and cocaine
It is
What remains after ruin
It is
The fluid used in photo booths
It is
Unfit for human consumption
It is
Poetry's presumption
That love will not turn to poison
On the palate
It is
How you cannot spit it out
It is
How you cannot spit it out
It is
How you cannot spit it out
It is
Agony

And the princess lies gagging
On the floor of a bathroom
She never asked to see.

Her lover leaves with the Autumn...

Limestone in water,
She crumbles.

The Death of Medusa

One winter...

Having grown tired of mortal men –
Who, lusting after dangerous liaison,
Come (sword in hand) to pound
Upon the mouth of sacred caves –
Fair-cheeked Medusa takes a mirror,
Turns stony gaze upon her own face
And hibernates.

Summer brings visitors...

Perseus, in want of her head,
Leaves disappointed
Proclaiming the 'whore of Sarpedon':
"Already dead."

Then comes the artist...

Reflected in ashen eyes, Medusa spies
Skin like dappled sunlight though pine trees.
The gods have favoured him with
A rare beauty and so too music:
He sings boldly, composes melodies
To spark heat in concrete limbs and
Medusa softens.

A Goddess, to Her Former Lover

If you can, forget me.

Throw out the baby
With the bath water,
Hack your nose
Stone slab straight
To spite the face
I loved,
Burn the photographs
Like bridges,
Darken not this door again.

You are dead.

And living flesh does not ache
For refrigerated touch,
I am too young to summer
In the Underworld.

Urania communed with the skies,
Flushed from hiding that sly fox
And Terpsichore
(Upon the rising cry of a hunting horn)
Danced like wild dogs.

At home, Polyhymnia watched the box,
Finished her chocolates and switched it off.

The Muses Prevent History Repeating Herself

Clio and he had history.
Of course, she had seen the spread,
Observed closely
The bedroom carpet – grown threadbare
In the steady progression
Of seconds since he left –
"He's in your head,"
Said her sisters and
Melpomene wept.

Thalia would not entertain it,
Laughed hysterically,
Conspired with Calliope
To spread rumours of infidelity.
Epic bitches both, they wove
Language like honey:
"For who would believe we two
Weak and feeble muses may
Wage war on love
Without humour and music?"

Erato believed,
But she lacked substance and when
Euterpe bashed out those bass heavy
Battle drums
She too was lost to love.

Mount Olympus Is Empty

CONTENTS

The Muses Prevent History Repeating Herself	9
A Goddess, to Her Former Lover	11
The Death of Medusa	12
Cassandra	14
Lament for a Fallen God	15
Digital Aphrodite	16
Lunesta	17
The Mother and the Mystic	18
Arachne	19
Hero Gets a Regrettable Tattoo	20
Pyromania	21
Poem to Hylas	22
Demophon's Burden	23
Brother of Monsters	24
Mistress Midas	25
Minotaurticulturist	26
The Pygmalion's Girl	27
A History of Dragons	28
Mount Olympus is Empty	30
The Very Last Love Song	31

Dedication

This book is dedicated to Jai Hadgraft and Frankie Dee Hadgraft. For the love, the lifts and for never asking me to get a proper job.

PUBLISHED BY VERVE POETRY PRESS
https://vervepoetrypress.com
mail@vervepoetrypress.com

All rights reserved
© 2020 Elise Hadgraft

The right of Elise Hadgraft to be identified as author of this work has been asserted in accordance with section 77 of the Copyright, Designs and Patents Act 1988.

No part of this work may be reproduced, stored or transmitted in any form or by any means, graphic, electronic, recorded or mechanical, without the prior written permission of the publisher.

FIRST PUBLISHED OCT 2020

Printed and bound in the UK
by ImprintDigital, Exeter

ISBN: 978-1-912565-43-6

Original Cover Photo: Rob Lycett

E. Hadgraft
Mount Olympus Is Empty

ABOUT

Elise Hadgraft is a graduate of The University of Edinburgh and now lives in the suburbs with her son, her dog and the rabbit.

Started in the basement of a cult complex on the outskirts of Berlin and finished over a year later in a suburban terrace, 'Mount Olympus Is Empty' is a brand new body of unperformed work by Elise Hadgraft. Influenced by half-remembered Greek mythology from her childhood, these pieces present a deeply personal insight into a mind struggling to rebuild itself after catastrophic collapse.

#HYSTPoet

Verve Poetry Press is a quite new and already award-winning press that focussed initially on meeting a local need in Birmingham - a need for the vibrant poetry scene here in Brum to find a way to present itself to the poetry world via publication. Co-founded by Stuart Bartholomew and Amerah Saleh, it now publishes poets from all corners of the UK - poets that speak to the city's varied and energetic qualities and will contribute to its many poetic stories.

Added to this is a colourful pamphlet series featuring poets who have previously performed at our sister festival - and a poetry show series which captures the magic of longer poetry performance pieces by poets such as Polarbear, Matt Abbott and Geraldine Carver.

Like the festival, we strive to think about poetry in inclusive ways and embrace the multiplicity of approaches towards this glorious art.

https://vervepoetrypress.com